Prelude:

My personal journey as a learner has provided a professional and retired lifetime of amazing opportunities and experiences in a wide range of educational settings – culminating as headteacher of a residential independent special school for students diagnosed as being on the autistic spectrum.

This was the cherry on top of a very rewarding career for me. The students taught me so much and I am indebted to parents, staff and professional colleagues for their dedication, wisdom, courage and always the hope with which together our achievements ranged from minute to momentous!

I invite the reader to share our personal and professional experiences and to celebrate achievements of students during their time at the school. Names in every case have been changed to protect the anonymity of everyone – except one. Mark has given me special permission to use his name as he too wants to join with me in this shared celebration praising our time spent together at the school and since.

In praise of difference – I hope to bring warmth, smiles and even a few happy tears when you read this journey of such a positive, rewarding set of experiences in my life.

Margaret Filley   July 2020

'It is not our differences that divide us. It is our inability to recognise, accept and celebrate those differences'

Audre Lorde, Poet.

I dedicate this book to the children, their parents and my staff colleagues who travelled my journey of wonder and happiness with me. But also to my son Mark whose diligence in proofing and excellent advice have been invaluable. And special thanks to my grand- daughter Abigail for designing the cover to celebrate the wonders of autism.

Chapter 1: Rules are rules...........but sometimes they don't fit the bill!

Every parent or guardian of an autistic child knows all too well the significance of a diagnosis and a Statement of Special Educational Needs as a precursor to gaining the right school placement for their son or daughter to access appropriate education and care. For some this is a nightmare experience. It certainly takes time and a huge amount of determination to achieve a place at an expensive and specialised provision. I am saddened that recently the media yet again drew attention to the number of autistic children not in school. I hope at least this celebration of the often remarkable insight my colleagues and I developed and some of the many simple successes we achieved together might give ideas and rewards to others. My story centres around Hope Lodge School, an Independent Special School for children on the autistic continuum managed by Hampshire Autistic Society. When the school had first been opened, by the parents of two children who were being given no education, I was told there was only one really important question at interview for any staff member – 'Will you love our children?' During my five years at the school everyone certainly did. We replaced anxiety with quiet calmness and a determination to manage change and help all our students access the world around them and enjoy fulfilment.

But first my personal journey and how I became totally absorbed in working with young people diagnosed within the autistic spectrum.

Unfortunately, my own education gave no opportunity for the development of thinking. At every stage through the primary and secondary phases learning was mostly rote and reliant upon memory. I remember very clearly, aged fifteen, an incident at the start of a science lesson. The teacher started to dictate for us to write down information. I had the quiet courage to put up my hand and politely say that she had our exercise books beside her. Her reaction was a huge influence on how I was to develop throughout my educational journey! I was angrily hauled to the front of the class to 'take the lesson'. The shame and embarrassment I suffered gave me a stark demonstration that a teacher is a role model for behaviour and I have always realised my job title was not 'teacher' but motivator. In fact that negative experience definitely turned in to a positive one for me.

Three years at teachers training college was the opportunity for me to be who I wanted to be. To think and decide for myself. I had to insist on taking pottery as a main subject ....but it was worth it. The hours spent throwing on the wheel and the ten attempts to fire a large moulded platter gave me patience and staying power, and my confidence grew when said platter was exhibited at the Three Counties Show in Malvern! I now never give up.

I had gone to this particular college in Herefordshire because my dear sister had been there 10 years previously. As a nine year old paying a first visit to this beautiful county and enjoying a 'Presentation Day' tea I sat opposite an erudite and quietly spoken lecturer who asked, 'and what are you going to do when you grow up dear?' The answer of course was to teach and follow the sister I had placed on a pedestal. Ten years later this same lecturer interviewed me for my place at the college and my future was starting to map out just as I'd hoped!

The first desire to challenge established educational procedures came during my final teaching practice. The class I was given for this contained one of a pair of twins. Upon enquiry I was informed that because the two babies had appeared either side of midnight on the 31st August one was therefore in my class and the second twin was placed in the year below as that birthday was in a separate school year.

I sincerely hope that such rigidity does not continue to influence extreme and disappointing decisions about learning and most importantly a child's personal well-being.

This experience has only helped to inspire me to challenge traditional expectations if they do not satisfy a child's learning nor emotional needs. Several experiences, whilst deputy head of a large primary school close to Reading University, influenced my future professional practice. The school frequently taught the children of visiting foreign students on bursaries from their governments. One such family was from Brazil and the three children spoke only Portuguese. The two boys attended a special unit for teaching English as a second language for several sessions each week. But the girl, aged seven, was considered too young for such intensive intervention. She was in my class and for the first story she wrote for me I let her down badly since I could not read Portuguese! However, she was obviously very bright and within just one month, by mixing constantly with her English peers, especially in the playground, her stories were written in English. Her two brothers on the other hand had failed to integrate and mix with other children at the school, nor make friendships. Consequently they made no educational progress in school at all. Do we as educationalists really know best?

During this time I was one of a small group of teachers chosen to study giftedness – how to provide suitable opportunities during the school day for children who were very intelligent and often unchallenged by the normal school curriculum. Two hours each week I was able to withdraw a group of eight children, whose ages ranged from 5 to 11 and who as a school staff we realised that perhaps the school programmes currently offered were insufficiently stimulating for them. I introduced topics such as probability – not normally found in a primary school timetable. It quickly became apparent that helping them discuss, listen to and accept the opinions of others in the group was of considerable benefit. Tolerance and patience needed to be encouraged as each child eagerly wanted to influence the rest of us with their views. This experience did encourage me to think outside the normal 'rules' and expectations for gifted children within our classes and our findings were shared not only within Berkshire but to a wider audience.

Before leaving to take up headship I was teaching the eldest children in the year prior to their leaving for secondary education. I had within the class group a very wide range of abilities and decided that one child who had a very high IQ would benefit more by having a personal daily timetable to ensure he was being stretched intellectually. He joined some of our sessions and was very well liked by the other children in the class. First thing each morning he and I discussed his tasks for the day which sometimes meant his mathematics being done at the end of the school day. Such was his focused attention that even his art work was a privilege to see. I include a drawing of an apple core which he did one morning whilst the rest of us were busy with our class work. He had a chameleon called Mavis who would occasionally be brought to school. And he was happily motivated and achieving in a different way to his classmates. This had been a first experience of accommodating difference in a mainstream school environment.

In the same class another, equally popular boy, had a very low ability level and I made him personal work cards for mathematics, focused mainly on manipulating numbers up to ten. He also had a large number square on his desk – big enough for him to actually put a finger on each number when counting. One morning he lined up with the others at my desk for help and when it was his turn told me that the number square was not big enough! The square practically covered his desk top so I asked him to show me.

He was right!

His current work card had moved him on to simple subtraction and the task in question asked him to take 9 away from 9. There was no zero on his number square....only the digits between 1 and 100. I was wrong and he taught me both humility and admiration for the simple courage that had enabled him to share his problem with me and teach me.

The journey to appreciating and accommodating 'difference' was accelerating! Being individual is an important right for any student. Being different is special and should be celebrated and encouraged.

Whilst headteacher of a mainstream primary school for five years I developed a personal fascination for children who were not able to access learning as easily or willingly as class teachers expected and who were often sent to me. I developed personal relationships with these children and honed my skills as a motivator. They were different in their behaviour or the way in which they were able to understand or access learning using the daily programmes of work across the school curriculum. But they were all learners and they helped me see the importance of uniqueness and acknowledge that every one of these different children were my personal professional responsibility.

Because behaviour had become the focus of my personal learning journey my career then took a different route. I was being asked to consider leaving the school environment and turn to advising and inspecting. But children and learning have always been my single dedicated passion. So, instead, my next role was to lead educational programmes for a group of ten pupils in a well established and much admired Language Impairment Unit attached to a large mainstream junior school in Hampshire. My new colleagues were Speech and Language Therapists....SALTS as they were endearingly called. This was my first introduction to the world of autism and a change in my professional purpose.

The apple core

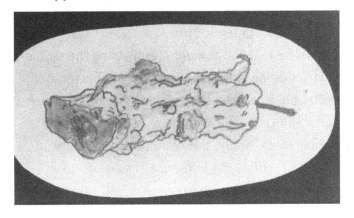

Chapter 2: So much more to communication!

Given the complexity of language, and the unique individuality of each child, what constitutes normal language development? This was the question at the heart of an investigation I undertook as part of my continuing professional studies. I had had the privilege of participating in 'Reading and the Language Arts', a course delivered mainly by the linguist and academic Professor David Crystal who told us he recalled someone expressing the opinion that acquiring language was simply a matter of imitation. However, the child development experts Sylva and Lunt (1982) found that deaf babies babble even though they cannot hear. Crystal (1976) describes the influence of parents on a baby's initial language experience, with the mother providing the first sensitive, supportive exchanges and encouraging turn taking, which is so necessary for conversation.

For the majority of children acquisition of language is a natural process. Where children have difficulty they live in a frightening and often lonely world. Vocabulary is very limited or even absent if the child has no intent to communicate. These children, identified by Harris (1990) as noncommunicating, may be remote and disinterested in communicating with others, as seen to varying degrees in many children diagnosed as autistic.

The resident Speech and Language Therapist at Hope Lodge School, (which was a specialist independent school for children with an autistic spectrum disorder where I subsequently spent five memorable years,) told me several years later that she had to make herself more interesting than Peter's twiddles! Peter had no speech and was constantly flicking coloured laces, being totally absorbed in watching them. Communication was not important to him but he was SO quick to notice anything new in his environment. Called to the door whilst filling a basket with potted plants at home, his mother recalled that seconds later, on her return to completing her indoor gardening project, Peter had eaten most of the plants. Sadly he was a frequent visitor to a very empathetic Southampton General Hospital.

As the teacher in charge of a Language Unit the influence of professional colleagues – Speech and Language Therapists – on my learning and future educational experiences was to be both profound and significant. The children in the Language Unit, where I happily now found myself, had all been diagnosed as having a severe language impairment. As such they benefitted from language programmes designed and monitored by two therapists, delivered both as regular individual sessions plus extended programmes suggested by the therapists and delivered by my team of six adults. As frequently as possible, the children also integrated with appropriate mainstream settings supported by the team. Some of these pupils had a diagnosis of autism, and, as lead coordinator, I was sometimes asked to visit a possible new pupil in their current educational setting to determine whether the Unit could be of benefit to their educational development. This was how I met Martin.

Martin was in a school for children with special educational needs, but his challenging behaviour was proving too difficult for the school to manage. His communication was heavily influenced by cartoon video speak which he watched constantly at home, using the pause button to fix and imitate a phrase or facial expression. He had actually been diagnosed as autistic by a very eminent educational psychologist whose notes stated that Martin had no understanding of numbers and could not draw. The diagnosis was given in her office with the parents present. When I visited the family home soon after Martin joined us the walls of his room were highly decorated by his paintings and above his parents' bed he had painted a clock showing 8.00 – this was the time his parents got up each morning. He was also teaching himself French from a video. Not bad for an 8 year old and sadly the psychologist forgot that autism is often very context specific.......so the assumptions she made were inaccurate. Her notes should have read 'he did not draw for me in my office' rather than he could not draw.

Very soon after joining us, and because his accompanying diagnosis explained he had no understanding of numbers, he and I were happily engaged with the introductory activities of sorting and matching – sitting as part of a group of four students and four assistants. Suddenly Martin exclaimed loudly 'No!' He got up and went round to a child sitting opposite who was working on subtraction of tens and units. Martin took a rubber and rubbed out the answer because it was incorrect. So, he did in fact understand numbers, including subtraction even upside down. Yet his diagnosis said he had no mathematical ability! I happily reassessed his programme for maths.

It was Martin who, together with another child diagnosed as autistic in the unit, influenced my understanding of the differences in the way these children learn. It taught me that we should make no assumptions, but simply observe and ensure we invite their interest and motivate them as learners.

The first week Martin joined the unit he and I went to a school assembly. Given his previous sheltered setting, plus the fact that his behaviour was often dramatic and challenging, being with 350 lively city children in the hall was going to be a very different experience for him. I sat behind him on a chair, close enough to predict and react to any behaviour. But he was perfectly controlled and sat beautifully. Assembly was always followed by morning play and the headteacher dismissed each class, one at a time, so there was a continuous stream of movement. I stood up and held Martin's hand and led him into the long corridor to return to the unit classroom which meant going down three short flights of steps. As I did so I said to him 'Well done Martin. Let's go back to the classroom'. He looked at me carefully, dropped his hand, turned around and held my hand again. I led him quietly and shame faced backwards to the classroom.

When working with autistic children I soon realised that ambiguity could create confusion and give rise to a 'different' interpretation to that which an adult would expect – as with the child who was asked by one of my team to take the register up to the Office. He did this.....but brought it back because he was not asked to leave it!

When giving talks on my experiences I always begin by holding up a white cup or mug – very handy if I have been invited to join the group for coffee! I ask them what I am holding. They will all without fail say 'a cup'. I explain to them that the answer I wanted was white – not a wrong answer, just a different interpretation of what we see.

Martin taught me so much more than I ever taught him. He was often anxious and things would be brushed off a table's surface in a wild sweep.................yet he quietly picked up and replaced everything carefully as his own personal strategy for calming down. No need for any of us to give him negative feedback, but rather wait until all items were in place and normal and offer him quiet praise.

One project involved our small group going outside, each child armed with clipboard and pencil, to produce a road survey – a count of people and vehicles passing by on the road. That afternoon Martin asked me if he could go outside to a small pond in the school grounds. He produced his own count of the forgs (frogs), logs, trees, worgs (worms), birds and bees. He also included a category for ponds.....and recorded one! This was entirely self initiated work.

I believe Martin showed us all that his under-achievement was because he had not previously been stimulated. He continued to have behaviours which challenged the staff and children in the large mainstream junior school and some of the children were worried by his outbursts though no one was ever hurt. He just expressed himself very noisily when he was anxious or frustrated. However, integration came to the rescue of his reputation!

Once a week I was required to teach a mainstream class for an afternoon. As the age was appropriate for Martin he accompanied me. He would take with him all he needed for the assignments I had given him. On arrival the apprehension of the children in the classroom was palpable. Martin sat quietly where I asked him to sit, usually close to me, and watched me write his list of tasks in a corner of the blackboard.......................then without a word of direction from me he became totally absorbed in his work. The children were enthralled and I explained that, like all of them, he came to school to learn, really enjoyed his work and was good at it – but that he was different. As they could see, he needed no further help, nor any reminders to get on and finish his tasks and work hard! Although Martin was not actually integrating into the shared programme of study this weekly experience gave an opportunity for the other children to see him very differently. Martin rose in their esteem.....and mine.

On my final day in the Language Unit there was a constant stream of children from the mainstream classes bringing me goodbye cards. That lunchtime Martin had had a challenging episode but was calmly starting the afternoon working alongside one of my team. He turned to her and said he wanted to make Mrs Filley a card. She found a pink

Martin's pond survey

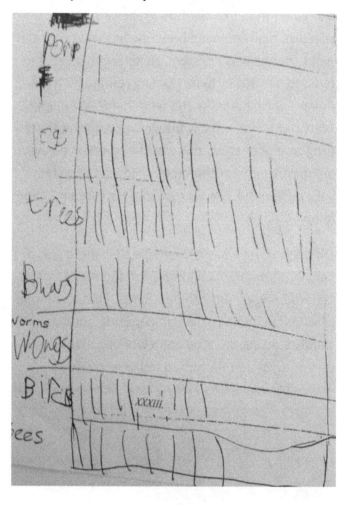

sheet of thin A4 card and folded it in half for him. He got up, collected a pair of scissors and cut along the bottom of the card.....he had wanted to make the card, not just write on it. His words were an amazing insight into his own autism and how he himself recognised he was different:

> Dear Mrs Filley
>
> Sorry I'm stupid
>
> And the worst therefore
>
> Distant   that was
>
> Bad   apaw apaw
>
> Make a fool
>
> I see now make
>
> A space madness   apaw apaw

A rather different goodbye message, but how perceptive he was. I still have, and treasure, that card.

Sadly, when I left the Language Unit and took up the role as headteacher of the autistic school,

Martin's behaviour became more challenging and he was too difficult to manage in that setting. But he followed me to Hope Lodge so I continued to benefit from the extraordinary differences and range of talents that he had.

A second child in the Unit often screamed. He was popular with everyone and the mainstream class teacher was always keen to invite him and include him in lessons. This was really appreciated by his mother who wanted him to be accepted and to benefit from as normal an education as possible. He was gifted musically and played the piano very fluently. He frequently played in main school assemblies. I did not need to be sent for because I could hear his screaming when it started several rooms and closed doors away! One day sitting down beside him in the classroom, having been greeted by a much relieved class teacher, I wrote his name on my notepad and passed it in front of him. He stopped screaming and read his name. I took back the pad, immediately accompanied by more screaming, and wrote 'please stop screaming as I don't like it' and passed it back to him. He stopped screaming, read my words out loud, looked at me – my face was always calm and expressionless when supporting behaviours – and he stopped screaming completely. After a few moments I smiled at him and said thank you.

Martin's good bye card which he 'made' by trimming off the bottom

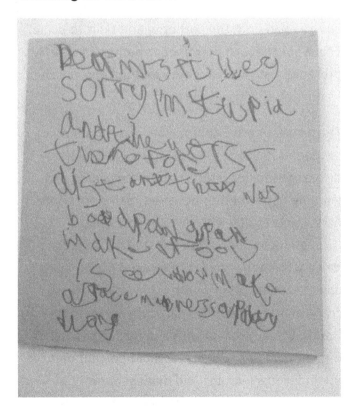

Another lesson learned – reduce the verbal communication and use non-threatening and calm facial expressions and gestures. Later at the autistic school whenever there was an episode of challenging behaviour and alarms had been sounded I would join the scenario, say nothing at all, but offer a calm, firm and consistent posture to reduce anxiety levels of everyone involved, staff and students, and it always worked. I never presumed to take over the situation though of course I had both the authority and skills to do so. This would have undermined my amazing staff. My presence just said 'I am here for you' and the child frequently checked I was there.

The time for verbal communication about an incident is never at the time it happens. Staff discussions follow later to share the causes and learning opportunities between themselves and, most importantly, with the student. Talking through the incident with the student is crucial to helping them recognise their own signs of raised anxiety and discussing with them choices they could make to avoid this particular event in the future. Being involved with and taking ownership of their own behaviours was an important part of our individual learning and management programmes. Language was key to this and with some of our students this meant pictorial images to help them make changes to their own lives by understanding and encouraging them to make choices.

I remember one girl who always sought me out when she was calm after such an incident. She implored me to let her stay at the school and asked me if I still loved her. She knew that the skilled and consistent approach we used was helping her recognise, understand and cope with her anxiety. After several failed school placements she knew we could help her. What success. I still have the pleasure of occasionally meeting this young lady who has worked 3 days a week for a large local supermarket for more than 13 years now. When I see her busily working in an aisle I gently say her name and hello. She turns and says 'hello Mrs Filley, can I hug you please?' I say yes and we do – sometimes in front of amazed shoppers. After mere seconds she will say 'I have to get on now' and will resume her task. I say goodbye and turn to any bemused onlookers and say proudly that the assistant was one of my pupils at my autistic school. I smile broadly and often get kind comments in return. I am so proud of this ex pupil who travelled a very difficult educational path – especially since she is one of twins and her sister is a nurse and married with a child. She has had to cope with so many disappointments and anxieties and yet is leading a very independent and happy life. Thank you to the staff of Hope Lodge and manager and all the staff of the supermarket for helping her to make this possible.

I have a family member with an autistic daughter who now has a job in a small retail outlet in a shopping mall and has recently just moved in to her own flat. Her mother is so proud of her determination and independence but sadly told me that her schooling had been very problematic. She asks why others do not see the differences that are such strengths in our children................they are totally reliable and trustworthy and there are so many jobs where their special gifts could be so valuable – especially if there is routine.

Time keeping is often an exceptional talent! All parents and those working with autistic young people know how rigid many of them are about timing and routines. This is both an important strength – reliability – and potentially a huge asset when leading a future life full of independence and opportunities.

Another boy in the Language Unit had to stay at home for a few days with an injury. This gave me a wonderful opportunity to visit and meet the whole family together after school one day. When I finally got up to leave, the boy looked up at the living room clock and said 'Mrs Filley is going at 5.46 and she arrived at 4.27'. Goodness, I doubt that the rest of us would have noted exactly when I arrived! What a unique gift to be so observant but also to remember so precisely – none of us as parents or educators had ever noticed this skill for detail before.

In three years working in the Language Unit I gained tremendous understanding and a range of skills as a result of working alongside Speech and Language Therapists: -three different methods of signing to communicate or enhance communication and pictorial reminders and cues to explain a schedule or routine and importantly to indicate and warn of change. I become more aware of and reflective about my verbal interactions with children. I also increasingly recognised the significance of behaviour as an important aspect of communication and key to gaining attention. I am indebted to these professionals for this huge leap in my appreciation of the individuality of each child. Having benefitted from teacher training which emphasised 'child centred' learning I moved from being driven by standard achievement tests to designing individual child-specific programmes which were updated sometimes hourly but definitely daily. Record keeping was so important as it not only evidenced learning and change, but absolutely defined a way forward for each child.

But what if language is not impaired.....................in fact it is wonderfully challenging because it is so advanced. I am sure, like me, many people have been entranced by the amazing numerical skills of the Rain Man, a sensitive interpretation of a real individual by the actor Dustin Hoffman. I was also lucky enough to have met and worked with a young girl who was equally gifted, but with words.

I was asked to assess her in a mainstream primary school. She had been diagnosed with Asperger Syndrome and was causing tremendous challenges for the school. She was nine years old and on the day of my assessment visit her class teacher was going to introduce the children to Haiku poetry. The young pupil had her own teaching assistant sitting beside her. The teacher wrote up a Haiku poem on the blackboard and began to introduce the class to the pattern it followed. The girl's arm shot up and she was saying 'miss, miss' and gesticulating wildly in excitement. The teacher stopped her explanation and asked her what she wanted to say.

She called out a hastily produced Haiku poem about her dog – no explanation needed by the teacher – the pattern had been interpreted and used within seconds. The teacher said well done and turned back to teach her class..................but again the girl's hand shot up. She had thought of another. At this point the teacher asked the teaching assistant to take her out of the room.

Needless to say the girl quickly came to Hope Lodge where she presented a very different challenge to us all – but the learning and rewards were incredible. She was in a class group of ten and two of the children were twins and had no formal speech, although they did make utterances. Our resident speech and language therapist quickly established that the girl had a huge fear of open spaces when, following an absorbing personal session with her, she asked her to go back to the class room. It was not the thought of joining the other children in her class that caused the huge and frightening behaviours outside my office......................it was having to go alone across the open playground to get there! No wonder in her previous school her behaviour had been so physical and dramatic...........it was an open plan school!

Despite having so little in common with any of her class mates this helped her become more reflective and understanding, demonstrating just how sensitive and caring she was. This had never been explored before. One morning she came to see me before the start of the school day. She was always so enthusiastic and she simply said 'Mrs Filley I want to write a poem about a child in my class'. I told her how delighted I was with her idea. The next morning she brought me the poem:

What's on your mind.

When I look into your eyes to find the sadness in your heart

I know you'd love to tell just how you feel

And when I hear your voice as you talk sadly to yourself

I understand that sadness is for real

        And I can tell the sun not to shine

        Or the wind not to blow

But there's one thing only you can tell me

That I need to know

What's on your mind?

Tell me now, I need to know

What's in your heart right now?

Deep down below

What's on your mind?

How do you feel!

Your heart beats heavily

But you just squeal

How do you cope as we sit together

Thinking of just what to say?

You open up your mouth but even then no words come out

Try telling me in your own way.

This incredible poetry repeats the refrain and has a further verse.

I felt very humbled by the insight of this then ten-year-old standing in front of me, let alone her skill with language. The next morning she was back again. This time she simply said 'Mrs Filley I want to sing it'. Fortunately we had an excellent music therapist on our staff who played a hugely important part in the programmes of our students. I also had several members of staff who played the guitar. The girl sang her poem to them and they accompanied her. How lucky we all were to have had the privilege of helping this young person with her special gifts. A DVD was made and sold for charity, the young girl proudly signing them herself.

Two months later she came to me again with a poem about – in her own words, 'Being on the Spectrum'. She called it 'Why' and it begins:

Why does it have to be us?

Jagged thinking in our heads,

What did we do wrong?

Some of us don't understand,

There is much more but this gave us all an important insight into the anxieties that this gifted girl had and the challenges she personally was facing. She only remained at the school for a short few months as she needed to be stimulated and given opportunities to develop her self-taught language skills. How lucky we were to have played a very small part in her educational life. A difference truly to remember and praise!

Chapter 3: Making a difference – small steps to quantum leaps!

The 'label' autistic was first introduced by a psychiatrist, Blueler (1916) to refer to a schizophrenic tendency to exclude the outside world. However, the first published account of autism was that of Leo Kanner (1943). Working in Baltimore he described children who were alert and attractive in appearance but with particular characteristics:

1) Socially aloof and indifferent;
2) Mute, or with repetitive or idiosyncratic speech;
3) Intensely resistant to change;
4) Having isolated skills with delays in learning.

The children at Hope Lodge School exhibited a range of these characteristics, but there was one aspect above all others which had given parents and educators alike a difficult challenge, resistance to change. Obsessive repeated behaviours and reactions to things in the environment were sometimes incorrectly thought of as bringing pleasure to a child or student. For this reason, and because outbursts of challenging behaviour could result if anything changed or stopped, those caring for and educating these children would let them continue – however inappropriate the behaviour or obsession might be. This was allowed to continue despite age inappropriateness or in some cases being unsafe.

Visiting a Special School in Sussex I was observing a child completing tasks from his morning schedule. He was compliant and well directed by his teaching support. He was then invited to go to his tray and take out his reward. I sat beside them both watching silently but with great difficulty. His treat was a box of matches. The teaching assistant took out a match, closed the box, lit the match and handed it to the boy. He let it burn right down to his finger tips and when it went out he laid the spent match on the wooden desk in front of him. He was allowed three matches in this way. I was horrified but it was not appropriate for me to intervene. However I made a severe complaint to the headteacher for allowing and fostering a 'reward' which was dangerous to the child and could also lead to a fire endangering the lives of others. The boy was obviously hypo-sensitive as he had no reaction when the flame touched his fingers. His obsessional liking for flames could so easily be transferred to other things which flicker....falling feathers or part-filled balloons, and as soon as he joined us at Hope Lodge they were! I am sure the school considered their actions a kindness to a child who liked to watch flames flicker - a reward for good work and behaviour. His compliance was misinterpreted as 'happiness' without understanding that obsessional behaviours continue because in their anxious world any outcome which is constant and predictable is preferred above all else.

On another occasion I visited a highly respected Special School which had achieved Beacon Status by OFSTED for outstanding practice. I was informed that a young boy of twelve years of age had no language and no skills, could do nothing for or by himself but was passive. I observed him having his lunch in the school dining hall. He didn't carry his lunch box and everything in it was handed to him by his teaching assistant - and of course she peeled his orange. There was no interaction from him apart from chewing and he didn't appear to give her any eye contact at all. The first session after lunch was art. He sat beside his helper who had pinned up a sheet of paper in front of him and prepared three jars of paint each with its own brush. She explained to him that they were going to paint together. She picked up his hand and manoeuvred it to a pick up a paint brush. He immediately averted his eyes to avoid any connection with what she was going to do. He continued to look away whilst she hand over hand painted a few lines on the paper – all the time talking to him but with no response at all. He was deliberately looking in my direction the whole time. He was actually choosing not to respond. The activity continued for several minutes but then suddenly the helper was called to another task. Immediately the boy's eyes reverted to the paper with its attempted picture. The paint was watery and was making rivulets down the page. He put his finger on one of these and started to draw with the paint. By himself!

He joined us very quickly at the school and the very first day he made a quantum leap! We had been unable to transition him gently as he seemingly had no skills. Two or three prior visits, together with Polaroid snaps as evidence to share and talk about at home, was our normal introduction for a new student. But this student just came with no rehearsal. We wanted his first day to have enjoyable activities and this included swimming. The class he joined was very small, just six children, all but two being boys. In the boys changing room the teacher asked them all to get changed. The newcomer – who had no speech – immediately raised his arms above his head! He had understood what he was asked to do and his reaction was to expect an adult to undress him. The teacher went over to him, gently put his arms down, took one of his hands and hand over hand tugged at the bottom of his t shirt and said again 'get undressed'. And he did! This was probably the first time he had ever undressed and dressed himself with minimal help and he had instantly proved that although he did not communicate he did understand. He also happily gave us all eye contact.

A few weeks later we were enjoying our annual swimming 'gala' which was in front of very appreciative parents and friends. All the children took part in some activity in the water and this young man was going to work his way down the complete length of the pool with his class. Suddenly, when he was right in the middle of the pool, he shouted and spun around several times, splashing and making verbal sounds. He treated us to a very special star display. And we were all happily clapping and cheering back to encourage him. He was free and doing things all by himself! What a transition. We all felt his joy.

Never be surprised!

On one occasion the need for change of behaviour had become very serious. A seven year old boy was losing speech, his general health was giving us all serious concern, and we agreed that changes to his diet would be needed. Case conferences were an important part of the management of our children. These included expert psychiatrists and psychologists from Southampton University, a paediatrician from Southampton General Hospital, as well as Social Services colleagues, and our own staff and therapists. But most importantly these also included parents or guardians.

This particular conference was called specifically to decide together how we should endeavour to change an obsessional diet of burnt toast and marmite for every meal, with no other type of food readily accepted. His mother explained that just occasionally he would accept a Yoplait yogurt and even more rarely he had eaten a Sainsbury's chicken nugget. However, being context specific and resistant to change, when she had taken the same frying pan, oil and chicken nugget to her sister's house for Christmas dinner he had refused the food. It had been cooked in a different kitchen. The paediatrician gave us all a serious warning about the long-term effects of such a rigid diet, so we had somehow to change this quickly to prevent further deterioration of his health and the potential risk to his life.

We all agreed to a trial period for one week. We would not offer him burnt toast and marmite at lunchtime for 5 school days. He would instead be offered a plate containing one small portion of each food type offered that day plus a Sainsbury's chicken nugget. We hoped that he would be sufficiently hungry and being offered no alternative choice would be tempted to pick up and try some other food type. He would have his burnt toast and marmite for breakfast and supper as usual. Because of his health problems we could not afford to extend this trial and we all agreed to meet at the end of the week.

The correct chicken nuggets were bought. Being a very valued and empathetic member of our staff team, cook was really happy to ensure his lunch plate looked enticing but with very little on it apart from that special ingredient we all hoped would tempt him to make changes. Without making it too obvious several of us followed his class to lunch and hovered to see what happened. Monday nothing; Tuesday, Wednesday, Thursday nothing. He just sat without making any attempt to pick up and try even the nugget.

Friday was different. I could tell before I arrived in the dining hall that something had happened. Cook had burnt the chicken nugget! She was heartbroken as it had also been the last one. But - he picked it up and ate it. The common factor of the burnt toast and marmite was BLACK! He was not taste specific at all as we had presumed. Happily this landmark mistake on cook's part changed his life. From then on everything offered to him at every meal was well-done to singed and within months he was voluntarily eating a whole range of food types and his health was definitely improving.

So never be surprised! This was a change that saved a child's life.

Inflexibility of thought and a rigid resistance to change dominated the behaviours of one young student. His control was so dramatic that he slept on the floor beside his mother each night. She told of him constantly waking her and was aware he was moving her head or other parts of her body during the night if she changed position. He was a very strong young man at twelve and had been attending a very successful autistic specific unit but they had been forced to exclude him because of dangerous behaviour. I agreed to accept him as a student but together with our paediatrician, who had an unparalleled reputation for understanding and managing autism, we argued that we did not want to rely on drugs to reduce or eliminate behaviours. It was essential that we observe and analyse how best to manage his anxieties and offer him an appropriate learning programme and learning environment. To do this we would need a team of specialists and assistants. We argued for, and secured resources for, a team of six adults to support and work with him for eighteen months. This successful negotiation undoubtedly changed this young man's future life opportunities, whilst of course making considerable demand on limited educational financial expenditure.

First the team. This consisted of a lead from a psychologist at Southampton University plus three of his staff and students. It was augmented by some of our own staff team who were keen to be part of this unusual project. Together they would analyse the student's behaviour each day using cameras. This provided evidence for the team to determine what factors raised his anxiety levels and what activities he seemed to engage with. During the day two staff worked with him or accompanied him through every activity, from assignments to eating and resting. Two others were constantly preparing his next activity or meal as any delay would raise his anxiety. The final two team members were recording and evidencing each and every behaviour exhibited by the student. At the end of each day the team, plus the lead Psychologist, analysed and discussed the student's reactions and agreed targets and preparations for the following day.

Working with this young man took courage and the two actually with him were often subjected to seriously challenging behaviour but quickly learnt that he needed to repeat the behaviours exactly and immediately. So whatever they had been subjected to they had to cope with an immediate action replay! Then he would run his hand down the arm of the person he had targeted. This was his way of accepting responsibility for his behaviour and more importantly we realised it was his way of saying sorry. We were so fortunate that one of these two amazing supporters was a former Royal Marine and well-practised in dealing with physical assault. He insisted on working with the young man and should be credited with the resulting success of changing the student's life chances because of his determination, calmness and courage.

By the end of the eighteen months we were able to reduce support to two adults and offer a much wider range of activities, including socially becoming a member of a class and therefore enjoying a wide range of visits into the community. Such was the progress that when he was 16, and because as headteacher of a mainstream school I had always wanted to offer opportunity to all children, I picked up the phone to Sparsholt College – a land-based college of Further Education. I asked the Principal if four of our students, accompanied by our staff, could be offered a morning session each week to include some animal management and some horticultural experience. The group of four was to include this young man, who, when we had accepted him into Hope Lodge, was considered the second most challenging student in the county. The Principal was delighted and the project a huge success for the students and also for staff at the college who benefitted from watching how skilfully our own staff worked with the four students, all of whom had complex needs. I was told the weekly visits were looked forward to.....................even allowing for the same questions being asked and the same routine being expected! One of the four immediately wanted to visit the pond area whenever he alighted from the school bus.

Because of Hope Lodge's success with this young man he is not reliant on drugs, and now lives in a bungalow with another young adult. He still requires twenty-four seven support but accesses the community, going shopping, visits and leisure activities. And of course we as a staff benefitted hugely from understanding the importance of evidencing and reacting immediately to the slightest increase in anxiety levels. This is a management ethic which has proved significant in many different management scenarios throughout my life – if something happens REACT. To ignore behaviour is to ensure it becomes accepted and possibly obsessional.

Every week during our school assemblies I would take a special box with me. It contained a surprise for a student who had made a significant achievement during the week....however small. I have a photograph of myself giving this young man his surprise. I am looking up at him (he was a foot taller than I was) and giving him his reward. He has his arms spread wide and held high and his expression is one of happy amazement – his mouth open wide! I think it shows a delighted and positive reaction to earning a reward.....probably for the first time in his life. A very special reminder of a momentous achievement which has pride of place in my home.

Alexander was seven years old when I visited him at his placement in an autistic specific unit in Wiltshire, and it was obvious why they could not manage his behaviours. He screamed – constantly. His parents were divorced and both had set up an identical room and routine for him when he was with either of them. As parents they were very anxious and when mother visited with me, together with her little boy, every action or behaviour was painfully felt by her. Her expression and especially her eyes looked so anxiously at her son and he was watching her intently.

He had never been away from home and we agreed to make his first school week with us just three days. The class-room staff were amazing and understood the feedback, positive or negative, that can be given by eyes. So Alexander had his own support assistant who sat beside him throughout his assignments – but with one BIG difference. She always averted her eyes. In fact she never looked at him. This made a significant and immediate difference........his screaming was much reduced in those first three days and eventually disappeared altogether. He had been feeding off the anxiety expressed by all his previous support staff and parents – through their eyes.

On the Thursday as soon as he arrived home his mother rang me amazed. He had not taken off all his clothes as he came through the front door. He had sat on the toilet for the very first time and he had just eaten a different biscuit from a different plate.

Such was the magic of Hope Lodge School and its amazingly sensitive, empathetic and professionally skilled team of staff. But more of that later.

4: Mark's story

I wonder how many ex-headteachers have had the privilege of a student asking if they might phone to keep in touch – for twenty years! Such is the privilege I have enjoyed by remaining in fairly regular contact with Mark. At first it was very regular – 7.00 on a Wednesday evening. But with exciting opportunities Mark's life is now so busy and rewarding that we still talk on the phone, email or meet for lunch, but only occasionally. I am delighted that he and his mother have allowed me to share his amazing life and the changes he has managed to make, enabling him to be independent and ever more successful.

Mark was already a pupil at Hope Lodge when I arrived. I knew him as a rather anxious and very talkative student but one who was eager to please and do well. His mother Sue came to work as a support assistant at the school while he was a student. She was one of two very dedicated parents who were so passionate about making a difference to other students' lives. In her own words she 'wanted to do my little bit and give a little of myself to others. I wanted to give the children the love and respect that I wanted for Mark'.

In the beginning life had been very difficult for Sue. Mark was her first child. She remembers he cried all the time and she knew he was different...... constantly banging his head on the floor and not making those first milestones which fill the memories of fond parents and grandparents alike. She was exhausted because the only time he was not crying was when he was asleep. Her Health Visitor could not help, but worse, made poor Sue feel like a neurotic mother! Sue did however discover that Mark didn't cry when he was in the swimming pool. By six months of age he was swimming like a fish.

By the time Mark was a year old, Sue, feeling completely exhausted, went to her doctor for advice. She told of Mark unwrapping a birthday present and only being interested in the wrapping paper.....twirling it round and round. It seemed as if he was in a world of his own giving her very little eye contact. And of course he cried. A lot. The doctor told her this was all normal but that there might be a problem with his hearing. His advice was to shut Mark in his bedroom and let him cry till he fell asleep exhausted.

Hearing tests followed but all gave normal results. However, Sue continued to be very anxious as Mark was not only starting to bite himself but also any other child he encountered. She felt very isolated as she couldn't mix with other mothers and their children because Mark's behaviour had become so unpredictable. In fact one mother told her that Mark was a horrible spoilt child and needed a good smack!

Returning to the doctor, Sue remembers that his focus seemed to be on her rather than on Mark. Sue admits that she was constantly in tears and felt so alone and useless. She looked very tired and had lost a great deal of weight. She asked if Mark could be referred to a paediatrician. Eventually, when Mark was about two and a half, he did have an appointment with a consultant. Sue remembers him being given various ability tests but after several sessions she was getting no answers as to why and how he was different. She had read a book by Tony Attwood, a British psychologist living in Australia and noted for his work on Asperger Syndrome. She realised that he was describing Mark and his behaviours and explained this to the consultant. He then went away and did his own research which happily resulted in Mark's diagnosis. Strange but true!

Happily, from the age of three until he was five Mark joined an 'opportunity group' for children with special needs. The relief for Sue was tremendous. At last she could talk about all the things that worried her...ask questions and just share thoughts with staff and parents alike. She also benefitted from a few hours respite and enthusiastically sought out coffee mornings, parents forums, seminars – in fact any opportunity to talk and get information. She remembers it felt like winning the lottery! From there Mark went on to attend a special school. All was well for the first two years, but with a change of class and a change of class teacher who failed to make a connection with, nor appreciate Mark's 'difference', things started to go very wrong. In hindsight Sue now realises that 'change' and the management of this has always been crucial to Mark's progress.

Mark was now eight and Sue was told by the county education team to look at all the special provision in their county and suggest what might be a more appropriate provision for him. She did, very thoroughly, including having to provide the education officials with evidence. She came to the conclusion that no provision offered in the county would meet Mark's needs and said so!

Her search widened to include out of county provisions and she found details of Hope Lodge School. Visiting the school she liked the small class sizes, small classrooms and a very high level of staffing ratio, which allowed students to be cared for and taught individually whilst remaining part of a small group. It answered all her deeply held desires for a calm and carefully constructed individual learning environment for Mark. But of course her own county was not willing to pay for him to attend a school in a neighbouring county, especially as this would mean him becoming a weekly border, adding considerably to the cost of his education.

Sue's determination kicked in! She literally telephoned County Hall every day, bombarding them with reminders that no school in the county could offer Mark what he needed and so they were letting her son down. Unbelievably she remembers well the day, a year later, when she received a telephone call to tell her funding for Hope Lodge School had been agreed. This was a turning point for mother and son but also for the county as Mark became the first student ever to receive 'out of county' funding for his education. A battle fought and won.

So in 1984, just before his tenth birthday, Mark became a pupil at Hope Lodge School. A turning point in his life.

I know from conversations with many parents of children on the autistic continuum that the anxiety, isolation and inability to cope felt by Sue is typical. Why should it be us? A total lack of empathy and understanding from others adds to a sense of personal failure as a parent. This is when 'difference' is at its most poignant and difficult phase. The child is not talking, not playing those delightful make-believe games so loved by parents and grandparents when a banana becomes a telephone with happy to and fro conversations. This anxiety, followed by the sheer determination needed to seek and find help and then get a diagnosis represents a mammoth journey for the parents. After that comes the long fight for a statement of Special Educational Needs to entitle their child to a placement at a specialised school like Hope Lodge. I am sure that simply 'staying the course' on this difficult journey for their child has defeated many. I often reflected that there must be many other deserving children who would never get to Hope Lodge perhaps because their parents were just not able to break through all of the barriers.

Sue tells of Mark loving Hope Lodge from the very beginning of his time at the school. But initially he found it difficult being away from home all week. It didn't help Sue that others said to her 'how can you let him board?' But she says that with the structure, clear boundaries, routine and management of any changes, and above all continuity, Mark went from strength to strength and thrived. But what did Mark think of all this and what are his memories of his time at the school?

Mark himself says that his six years at the school encouraged him to try new foods and new activities. He was made to feel much more confident because of the love and support he was given. In particular he gives credit to the Speech and Language Therapist who helped him gain confidence in speaking to other people. Mark had always provided lots of examples of his ability to say things as he saw them with no appreciation of the emotional appropriateness of giving his opinion. His mother remembers when he was seven and in Woolworths at the pick 'n' mix counter, happily filling his bag. A stranger said to him 'Oh you like your pick and mix young man'. Mark replied 'Yes I do. Why are you so fat and not straight up and down like my mum?' Fortunately the lady said what a sweet boy he was, but mother was worried about the future when perhaps 'sweet' would not be a first response from an unknown person to Mark's bluntness. A few years later at Hope Lodge one of the staff had dressed up as Father Christmas. Entering Mark's classroom and being introduced to the children with his bulging sack of presents Mark responded 'No it isn't. It's Keith because I can see his shoes'. An eye for detail that is so much more acute than most of us – and a strength that can be harnessed.

Language therapy helped Mark understand the consequences of what he might say. This is often difficult for children on the autistic spectrum as they may not have the same emotional reactions to a situation as the majority of us. But they can be made more aware and taught a variety of options through either individual or group therapy sessions. Once a week all classes throughout the school had an hour of language games. These were devised and suggested for each group by the therapist and provided a happy social experience of using language appropriately. Mark remembers these sessions with affection and confirms their effectiveness by commenting that they made him much more confident speaking to other people and taking his turn.

Mark also enjoyed trying new activities. We were lucky because the school was in a large and bustling city which offered endless opportunities to arrange visits, experience and join in a wide variety of events and sports. The children were allowed to use the gymnasium and field at the neighbouring grammar school. Some children also joined taught lessons accompanied by a member of Hope Lodge staff where this was appropriate. Our sports day was hosted by this school and always such a happy day for students and families. We had an annual picnic and barbecue organised by the kitchen staff at a local countryside beauty spot. Hope Lodge was given use of the city indoor swimming pool and a local sports centre offering bowling and a climbing wall. And of course they all went shopping. We took our students out in our minibuses as frequently as we could each week to encourage appropriate behaviour, strengthen them physically and also to overcome anxieties to dogs, people, and movement, and accustom them to the hurly burly of a normal busy environment. And it worked – Mark acknowledges how important this immersion in the real world was for his confidence and his ability to cope with anxiety. 'Try something new' is what he still constantly tells himself and this new-found courage and determination continues to make a tremendous difference to his life.

At Hope Lodge School one of our residential facilities, known as the Cottage, was specifically organised to encourage life skills for a small group of students who were likely to embark on more independent life styles. Mark so enjoyed these experiences and has fond memories of this aspect of school life as an important milestone. He felt ever more independent. He remembers enjoying 'taking it in turns to wash and dry up after a meal; laying the table for breakfast or the evening meal; taking it in turns to empty the bins, cleaning and keeping our home tidy and presentable; and being able to stay up later'. I wonder how many other teenagers would see these activities as enjoyable? All students benefitted from these experiences and I remember one evening watching the child mentioned in an earlier chapter as having a preference for black food. He was preparing vegetables for soup for supper. Change? Yes, often a huge problem for our students but we moved them all on to lead much fuller and healthier lives. We were in a city and exploited it to the benefit of not only the students but also their families who had encountered many episodes of difficult behaviour in the past. They were so grateful that we frequently took their child into the busy world outside school, enjoying and being accepted by others in the community. We did not want the school and its residential facilities to become the only environment for these children. Our goal was to help them recognise and manage their anxieties for themselves in a variety of normal settings.

In one of my previous school settings I had run a junior Neighbourhood Watch Club together with the local police officer. The aim was to encourage responsible behaviour and an understanding of work and play as members of a happy caring community, so why not introduce this into my new educational environment? Especially as road safety, personal safety, and right and wrong were important lessons for our students who, like Mark, would one day be able to access an independent lifestyle. Hence the Look Out Club began.

I have always benefitted from close working relationships with Hampshire Constabulary through my community-based Neighbourhood Watch activities. I could therefore request police colleagues to visit and engage with the students, which was so beneficial for both parties, I believe. For example, many autistic children are very anxious about dogs – their unpredictable and rapid movements cause increased alarm, making a simple family pleasure of walking together in a park a nightmare experience. So the dog unit paid us a visit and provided a wonderful display in the school playground. The children who would have been most sensitive and anxious stayed inside and watched through windows. But others enjoyed the chance of even touching the two dogs and talking with the trainers. The Marine Unit also gave us a presentation which was informative and entertaining for the students. They brought ropes and fenders and showed spectacular film footage of some of the ways they kept the Solent and our waterways safe for us all.

In our Asperger specific unit for 16 to18 year olds we had, for example, a young man who had three incidents in rapid succession, involving the police. He returned home to his foster parents at weekends and holidays, and loved to go out into the busy town and resort of Southsea as often as possible. He was different because at 17 years of age he was especially kind and thoughtful. For example whenever I visited this unit he would always escort me out to my car and insist on opening my driver's door for me to get in. Impeccable manners but sadly they were to cause two of the incidents!

On the first occasion he had been picked up by the police and taken to the station for questioning but had been wrongly identified and accused. This created a win-win opportunity for the staff not only to support the student through the anxiety caused by this experience, but to offer to meet and share knowledge with the police involved, who had found the experience baffling as the answers and behaviours they received were not as they expected. So a valuable outcome for all.

The second incident occurred because the student liked to go up to elderly people and ask if he could help carry their shopping. One such person complained to the police – so he had a second visit to the police station. Once again staff worked with the police to explain and help with strategies when dealing with an autistic person. For the student we needed him to understand that some adults might not welcome his kind offer. For his personal safety we needed to make him more aware and cautious. But the third incident was a more serious issue and a learning opportunity for all ten students in the unit and ourselves as staff.

The students in this unit frequently had opportunities to shop, attend the local city college or for some other reason to access the nearby vicinity by themselves. On one such occasion this student returned with an elderly homeless man who was bleeding. He of course had felt pity for the man and hearing that he had no friends and nowhere to go wanted to take care of him. This meant calling once again on our local police, this time for advice, and also to seek medical advice because of contact with body fluids. Once the elderly gentleman had safely departed the staff began an unexpected teaching opportunity to help all the students understand the consequences of some of the choices they might make. This act of kindness had possibly put all staff and students in danger but had been so charitable in intent. The Look Out Club continued to provide an interface between the school and our local police teams.

Apart from activities for the whole school group the Look Out Club met weekly. Those who came had volunteered to be members of the club and we felt we needed to identify our small but enthusiastic group by designing a logo. A happy clown face became the agreed image and featured on homemade badges for us all. We then decided to go one step further and put the logo on to a t shirt. These were produced and Mark, who was a very enthusiastic member of the club, often leading conversations about 'danger stranger' and crossing roads safely, had a very outspoken reaction!

Sue remembers Mark telling her

'I went to see Mrs Filley today about Lookout Club.'

She replied 'Oh lovely Mark, was that ok?'

Mark's response was 'Well, I told Mrs Filley that I like the Lookout club but I don't want to wear that stupid shirt!'

'Oh right Mark, do you think that was the right thing to say?'

'Well Mrs Filley said I could always speak to her if I had any concerns, so I told her'.

Mark and his mum sometimes replay this story together and always end up laughing. For my part I am so proud of encouraging Mark to speak out when things are inappropriate.....and at the age of 15 he felt quite rightly that our image was too immature. This confidence in speaking out when things are not right resulted years later in Mark speaking out on behalf of both himself and four other vulnerable residents in a small residential environment. The care staff were swearing and in

Mark's opinion being unkind to his friends who had a range of physical and learning handicaps. His complaints were taken seriously and all residents found new accommodation. When Mark's finances were transferred to a new bank closer to where he currently lives it was discovered that a considerable amount of money had been taken from his account. This was the result of the carers insisting on knowing the personal banking details of all five vulnerable residents and was further proof of their criminality. Thanks to Mark telling the authorities about his concerns the outcome for all five residents was good – a lesson for life learnt through the Look Out Club.

Mark is now very happily living in a different part of the county. During this experience both Sue and I offered and provided encouragement and support because the process of dealing with the complaint, together with the unhappiness caused by the care staff, increased Mark's anxiety considerably. We are both SO proud of Mark undertaking and surviving such a difficult personal experience. But of much more importance he is proud of himself because however painful he knows he did the right thing for himself and his friends. And his confidence continues to grow.

After leaving Hope Lodge at 16, Mark attended Southampton City College where he had opportunities to study computers and a short business course. He also experienced more practical skills such as bakery and brick-laying. A few years later his family moved to Polperro in Cornwall and Mark was able to capitalise on these new skills and especially his eagerness to access the world about him.

I also remember him describing his enjoyment working at a Cancer Research UK charity shop in Looe. He explained to me that he needed to feel he was paying people back for the grants and opportunities he was being given. This responsible attitude is a true indicator of the determined 'right from wrong' attitude which characterises Mark. He was to work in this charity shop for 7 years and during that time he studied for and succeeded in attaining 2 National Vocational Qualification awards in serving customers and financial management. He was responsible for taking money to the local bank and from our regular telephone conversations it was obvious that he was enjoying all these new opportunities.

In April 2016 Mark received a Flame of Hope Award presented by his manager in the Cancer UK Charity shop in Looe. Mark tells me it was such an achievement for him and he felt so proud. He was given a pin badge, a framed certificate and a DVD from the charity headquarters, congratulating him for his brilliant volunteering over a ten year period. He says that he was one of only two to receive the award that year from an original list of 798 applications nationally.

Being a tourist area Mark also found friendship as well as work in the local caravan holiday sites. He socialised and made new friends, though of course none of them permanent as both holiday makers and staff were often changing or disappearing. But this was a happy and successful learning opportunity in his life. The family then decided to move to Tenerife. Mark was given the choice of going too, but after much shared deliberation, myself included as a 'sounding board', Mark decided he wanted to stay. Social Services quite rightly questioned the value of Mark remaining in Polperro which was a seasonal resort and did not have a peer group that he could share his time and interests with all year round. He chose to return to Southampton where he had friends from his previous life in the city and the school and was found supported accommodation.

This was obviously an anxious time for Sue and she and I kept once again in frequent touch with Mark so that he could share his anxieties and also his successes. He was travelling happily on buses and trains and was later to extend his travel experiences to regular visits twice a year to Tenerife. Because he is so organised and makes excellent use of computer, phone, timetables and always his support staff, he is now able to plan excursions including his scheduled visits to his mother, which is a tremendous leap in independence........well not quite. The staff at his current home setting utilise formal assessment procedures which they work through with him to ensure his safety, timing, and alternative arrangements should delay be a factor. In fact they enable him to accomplish the most challenging of journeys and events. Mark organises his own flights from Bournemouth airport and arranges his taxi transport. He shares these details with the staff who support him. But he also likes to go to national concerts and conventions on his personal enthusiasms. One such journey to Cardiff meant a three hour train journey which included a change of train service at Reading Station. The convention lasted two hours and the return journey took a little longer – four hours this time. All achieved in one day's excursion. I know that Sue joins me in the pride and joy which we both share because of this incredible determination and confidence which Mark now has.

In his new setting Mark is of course working in a charity shop, but not locally this time. He needs to travel and he explained to me that he goes by train in the morning but because he felt uncomfortable with some people he met or saw on the return train journey he always returns by bus in the afternoon. Proof once again that Mark has learnt to 'change' details if necessary and he can make choices to ensure his personal safety and wellbeing. Walking down the local street with him is so rewarding as strangers unknown to me will stop and speak or even call 'hello Mark' from across the road. He is really happy and settled thanks to his excellent accommodation and the staff team. He is given as much independence as possible, he offers help to other residents who have limited capacities and skills and has a very organised weekly routine. My planned visits need not only to avoid the two days spent at the charity shop but also Mondays – shopping day, and Tuesdays – laundry. When we go to one of his favourite local places for lunch he is so very popular.

What a success story!

I recently introduced Mark to his local Police Chief Inspector, as I believe he could offer help to other vulnerable young adults, especially as he has such a clear understanding of right and wrong. Not only did Mark insist on buying us both coffee, but also (having sent the Chief Inspector to sit down after a tussle between them both as to who would pay) bought the surprised police officer a cake! There may be future opportunities for Mark to share his achievements and offer support to encourage others to make appropriate choices and take actions for their personal safety. I should so like to see him become a champion for others.

Chapter 5: The magic of hope

An Inspector who headed the county autism forum paid a day's visit to Hope Lodge School. Before she left she said to me 'If only I could have just one of your staff!' It was they, who, together, changed and improved the lives of so many of our students. My role was simply to be their champion as well, of course, as being the champion for every student. I felt It important to celebrate success rather than dwell on the negatives of difficult behaviour – so often the reason for pupils joining our school.

One of my first contributions was to display art work along the walls of the entrance hall so all who visited could enjoy it – the students too of course. I was firmly told it would be torn down or spoilt.................it never was. The students were fascinated seeing their work on the walls. The displays attracted a lot of attention as well as greeting any visitor with the wonderful examples of what our students could do.

But the second change I insisted on very early during the tenure of my headship was to reconsider the constant locking of all doors. It meant every staff member carrying a bunch of keys and the students watching while they were locked in or out of the building or any and every individual room. Key codes were not effective as with excellent peripheral vision a student could memorise the code sequence immediately! This locking procedure raised everyone's anxiety level which was surely counterproductive given the need for us to reduce anxiety in all our students to help them cope with the unexpected events in life. I also felt it announced firmly to everyone – including the students – that they were unpredictable so beware!

Staff agreed with my concerns and we trialled a successful period of not locking doors unless there was a specific safety issue which needed to be addressed. This procedure was a great success with everybody, including visitors who appreciated the calm, welcoming atmosphere – and frequently said so. But the changes were supported by very rigorous and detailed safeguarding procedures, where and when necessary, including the use of alarm bells throughout the school when required. We all enjoyed a much freer, more relaxed environment. Students were actively encouraged to recognise when their anxiety levels were escalating and could let themselves out into the playground and relax with their personal chosen activity to calm themselves down before returning to the classroom. My office overlooked the playground and I had a constant visual overview of such events together, of course, with the classroom staff monitoring the student. The students gained in confidence and, more importantly, moved on to being helped to react positively where events or stimuli had previously raised their anxiety. Better still they were learning to control their own behaviour and reactions rather than us – a hugely important area of personal learning to allow them to develop independence and be better placed to happily access the world around them. My bonus was that the swivel chair at my desk was a huge attraction! Freedom of movement for students meant that, having been asked to take the class register to the main office, they could stop off and come into my room –where the door was always open and inviting unless closed for a confidential meeting. I often had to vacate it and let a young person have a few turns and gaze out over the playground! A wonderful way to bond with all the students at their invitation.

A visiting school inspector once challenged the fact that during play times students were not set personal programmes of activities. The children all had favourite and repetitive activities and I explained firmly that as our expectations were for learning periods to be carefully structured and detailed (to help them move on and develop both their educational ability and their social and personal skills), playtimes were sacrosanct and the activities chosen by the individual student. They all deserved to 'switch off' and be themselves, doing what they enjoyed most. I remember listening to a young adult speaking about her amazing achievements as a person diagnosed as having Asperger Syndrome. Both academically and through her blossoming career she was achieving great recognition and success. However when she went back to her flat after a busy, often high profile day, she loved nothing better than simply to flick pieces of paper which was her personal way of winding down privately.

Subsequently as an Ofsted inspector – one of few with autism-specific experience visiting other establishments for children on the autistic spectrum, I sadly noted that sometimes even shoes were taken off and placed outside classroom doors, all doors locked and worst of all the classroom walls left totally blank. When enquiring about this extreme lack of stimulation I was told it was because the children were hyper or hypo sensitive to visual and sound stimuli and needed a safe, secure environment. The justification seemed to be 'don't introduce or do anything for or with these children in case it upsets them'. Keep them in a predictable 'cocoon'!

At Hope Lodge we took a very different view because our parents unanimously agreed that they wanted their children to be accepted in the normal world – not locked away in a sanitised environment devoid of stimulation. We wanted to help them develop and change, and be able to access age-appropriate activities wherever possible. Postman Pat – such a favourite and much repeated fascination for young autistic children – is simply not age appropriate as a favourite tune when you are a teenager! With the gradual introduction of a wider range of melodies (I remember The Blues Brothers becoming a favourite!) and activities we moved every child on from the obsessional 'bubble' where they were trapped simply because everyone thought the constant repetition brought them happiness. To deny, remove or change would induce severe behavioural outcomes! So best avoided. Not so – as with the little boy who was given lit matches as a reward which was happily and easily substituted by something more appropriate.

Our aim for all our students was to help them manage change – in case the bus is late or the train does not arrive at all. We wanted our students to be able to deal with the challenges they had yet to face. As someone once said – happiness is not the absence of problems but the ability to deal with them (anonymous). The students at Hope Lodge were all very different but my desire as their headteacher was the same for these young people as it had been in a much larger mainstream school – opportunity and motivation for every one of them even though the starting point was so varied.

To achieve this we needed to monitor and recognise what induced anxiety in any individual child. And to ensure the gradual overcoming of the often extremely challenging behaviours which could result from their being close to, seeing, hearing or touching the cause of the anxiety. We wanted each child to progress as they matured rather than being kept in an obsessional and inappropriate vacuum – a setting devoid of excitement and opportunity. Our detailed individual management programmes for each child, the result of consultation with staff, professional colleagues and most importantly our parents, helped them to overcome any dramatic reactions and to tolerate more and more of the busy world around them. Both Mark and his mother Sue champion the benefits of our passionate intent as a school.

I believe our success was in offering students and their families hope. The families had faced years of embarrassment, worry and often hostility and we needed to change this to optimism, comfort and understanding – hope. When they arrived for the first time, often very anxious, I would show everyone the message (written in invisible writing) above my door – 'no problem, just an opportunity'. The significance of the word hope had a tremendous influence on us all. As a staff team we sought to be **H**appy, **O**ptimistic, **P**ositive and patient and to offer an **E**clectic and effective programme of study, opportunities and experiences to motivate our students as learners. **HOPE.** I was always so appreciative of, and inspired personally, by the name of our school – Hope Lodge

Many of the students came to us from special units for children with autism and had been offered educational programmes based upon current and highly regarded methodologies for children on the autistic continuum. We had all received training in these approaches, but I also had considerable experience from my mainstream background of motivating children in a variety of ways.

Professional studies had allowed me to focus upon the autistic spectrum studying in particular how learning is different for these children and how this might best be evidenced. Characteristics can include communication reluctance or difficulties, inflexibility of thinking, dislike of change as well as cognitive difficulties. I concluded that observation was key to discovering the unique approaches needed for an individual child – capitalising on obsessional interests. Educational programmes should offer a variety of methodologies rather than just one. We were proudly eclectic in the education and management of our students. And it worked!

As an example, music can universally charm, calm and provide entertainment at so many levels.......classical to hip hop, especially for children on the autistic spectrum. A first happy memory of Hope Lodge was the wonderful concerts. All our children took part. Whether moving to the rhythm, making musical sounds on instruments or singing along, the enthusiasm of the children was obvious. Added to which they were taking part in a social group activity with mum, dad and grandparents watching enthralled. I always warned them to bring a large handkerchief! Most of the students would never have participated in such a group activity before and the pleasure this gave everyone was immense. Parents could be so proud – and were! Music had pulled down the barriers of reluctance to participate. Once a week we had a school assembly. This was always quite a noisy affair with lots of gesturing and moving about going on. The words to a song were always on the wall, large enough for all fifty six students to see and many to be able to read. We sang and clapped our hearts out, accompanied by piano and guitars.

One boy I was asked to assess was proving too difficult to manage in his current special school placement. I found him in a room of his own with his teaching assistant..........he was not allowed to mix with other children as he was considered dangerous. He had no speech and a very limited range of activities. Once again I was told he had no understanding of numbers. But he had a piano in the room and he played Vivaldi by ear! Such an amazing gift. The only other information I was given was that he loved to watch washing machines and spin driers.

How could we use his gift with music to open up learning new skills, including being an active member of a group? Our concerts and our 'added value' ingredient, music, provided the answer.

When he arrived at our school he was given music therapy sessions with our therapist who was herself a trained professional pianist and had become an important asset to our staff team. She knew each child's favourite instruments and when one arrived at the start of a session this selection of instruments was ready and waiting. Her method was to gently accompany the child's strumming, banging or blowing and create a two way 'conversation' using their combined musical sounds. It was a musical way of replicating the sensitive exchanges in turn taking when a mother is first encouraging language skills with her baby. It also built up confidence and social skills. And this new boy was immediately participating in a meaningful activity with someone else.

This particular boy, with his incredible gift and love of music, developed readily in so many ways. No understanding of numbers? This was easily overcome by using pictures of washing machines and spin dryers. If he was given the chance to bring the class register to the school office he would linger in the laundry on his way back to class............absorbed by the spinning motion of the drier which was constantly in use. Later on, staff interested him in the mechanics of how the machines worked and he was even invited to a factory to see how they were made. But most importantly we offered him access to a full and busy school day as one of a class group. Because he was also a residential placement he could participate in the many activities which the residential staff organised – bowling, swimming, walking and shopping.

Ben was a boy who derived great comfort from music and still does. His mother Tilly is ever grateful for the calming effect of one staff member strumming his guitar or playing the piano. Ben would sit quietly and listen and then attempt to make music for himself –starting a conversation through simple shared sounds. One year, just two days before Christmas, while Ben was home from school he suddenly asked for a 'rain guitar'. He had never before asked for anything at all. For a surprised mother it was obviously vital to track this down, even though Christmas Day loomed close, rather than disappoint him. Tilly contacted the Family Services Officer at Hope Lodge and she in turn contacted other staff – all on holiday and preparing their family Christmases. But no one had any idea what a 'rain guitar' might be. The next day, Christmas Eve, at a friend's house, Ben sat looking at an Argos catalogue and suddenly said 'rain guitar'! It was in fact a normal instrument but had a tear drop shape on it. Problem solved! Tilly managed to get one for Christmas Day! As a young adult Ben's placement success has depended upon the understanding and necessity for staff to provide musical instruments for him. Without this vital ingredient in his life some care scenarios have sadly failed to provide an environment where Ben is happy and able to express himself through his love of music. Many years later he still recalls the names of staff at Hope Lodge who helped discover this important ingredient in his life and happiness.

The OFSTED report on Hope Lodge dated September 2001 noted a strength as - 'the way the school looks after its pupils and students is very good and this is reflected in the very caring ethos of the school'. During the same school year we also achieved award status for Investors in People, demonstrating our determination as a staff team to work collaboratively and use every experience to enhance our own personal expertise and understanding. I believe that humility and an eagerness to learn were common factors for us all. But we emphasised the need to watch and listen and then to analyse what we saw together as a team. And never be surprised! Sue as both a mother of one of our pupils and also a member of staff, says that as a parent her maxim was....be positive because there is light at the end of the tunnel. But as a member of the staff she simply 'had to be prepared for anything'! Another parent has told of no longer feeling a neurotic mother of an out-of-control child once her son joined the school after a long battle for placement. Her anxieties were reduced because the staff team now responsible for her son did not condemn nor suggest retribution for his challenging behaviour. This instant and huge relief was accomplished after a relatively short introduction to the school. How was this achieved?

Hope Lodge was built upon the principle of a total school and community approach to the education provided for our students and their families. We offered a wide range of accredited approaches to working with autistic and Asperger children and young people – we were proudly eclectic using no single methodology to the exclusion of others. We were interventionist in that we quietly and with determination undertook to change inappropriate behaviours, likes and dislikes, rather than accepting these were 'preferred' responses of a young person. They may have become the norm simply because an outcome was predictable and offered the child control of his or her surroundings. Repeated behaviours did not signify they were liked or indeed made the child 'happy'. As a team I believe we were non-threatening and as leader I undertook to challenge any member of the staff team whose reactions I considered to be inappropriate as soon as I either saw this for myself or had it reported to me. Immediacy in our world was vital. We encouraged self-esteem in both staff members and students. Staff training was a continuous process so we could all be confident of a united approach. We could 'lean on the team'! But most fundamental to our approach, and I believe our success with all the students, was the partnership we established with every parent.

The Warnock Report of 1978 had emphasised that the successful education of children with educational special needs was dependent upon the full involvement of the parents who had a profound influence on the child's educational progress. Parents can offer an intimate and valuable insight into the child and should be encouraged to do so. I firmly believe this ensured a 'togetherness' between school staff and parents which made a huge difference to mutual understanding and purpose between us all and inevitably the continuous and often rapid progress of the student.

Where we could help eliminate difficulties at home we would develop a programme with the parents so that visiting the dentist, buying new shoes, travelling by plane, each and every difficult family event could be shared, discussed and have the support of an experienced team who knew their child. Practice visits to include the parents could easily be arranged so that the parent could comfortably 'mirror' the methods, language and postures of the staff member. We had a secret and magical ingredient in our team to oversee and engage with parents constantly.

Our Family Services Officer was a huge and significant asset for staff, students and parents alike. A full-time member of the staff team (plus lots of optional overtime!) she had an office of her own which was always busy. One parent has told me that Brenda saved her sanity on many occasions. The school strongly believed in working together with the home, parents and guardians, to ensure a comprehensive and consistent twenty four seven management programme. To achieve this it was imperative to include and encourage the home setting, both to share issues but also to adopt changes and behaviour management opportunities the school discovered helped their child progress. Our aim was not to shut our children away but to help them tolerate and access as many opportunities as possible. We were lucky that our school was in the heart of a thriving bustling city – Southampton, which offered exciting daily doses of real life.

Tilly has a special memory of the organised support 'over and above' expectation, at a time when she was having chemotherapy. The help Brenda gave her and support she put in place for Ben because of changes to his routine were invaluable at a very difficult time for the family. Two members of staff arrived much earlier on a Monday to meet Ben and give him breakfast so that Tilly could be at the hospital in Guildford in time for her weekly treatment, His routines were kept as normal as possible during this time, with his mother still managing to collect him at the usual time on a Friday. The only difference was that Brenda was there too – to carry Ben's heavy bags back to the car! The move for Ben to a residential school had been difficult for both parents even though they had fought so hard to get him to the school. Tilly remembers it 'was a huge emotional hurdle'. She says that Brenda saved her sanity and as parents, they will always be grateful for the hugely supportive staff team during Ben's time at the school.

There is no doubt in my mind that a combination of team work.....the team to include the parents of course ....and the optimistic and positive interventions that we adopted had a huge influence on the progress of the student and the family's ability to lead a more interesting and even adventurous social life outside school. I was told of the excitement and achievement when one student flew on holiday for the first time. Another mother, coming to terms with a diagnosis of cancer and of course so anxious for her non-verbal twins, both autistic, was suddenly sent to the front of the waiting queue for her new Morgan sports car because of her circumstances. She shared with us the joy that, roof down and both twins squeezed into the car, every time they passed a cyclist one of the twins squealed so happily, not quite de-seating the rider who invariably realised and joined the fun too! Buying shoes, shopping, visiting museums and bowling or even ice skating suddenly became possible because through our Family Services Officer developing such close bonds with all our families, possible problems could be shared and team expertise enlisted to put together a workable solution.

Making a difference – and we did!

Chapter 6: Vive le difference!

For me there is an interesting educational paradigm. I trained as a teacher – yet I am truly a learner. I believe in reversing the emphasis because children, especially those on the autistic continuum, have taught me so much about how children learn. I hope I can now share a few of the ways I believe we can all make a difference to these children. They may be small steps, but I appeal for educational statisticians to enable small and even miniscule steps to be valued and evidenced even though they do not currently figure in the extensive range of standard school tests.

Behaviour is a key indicator to the emotional and I believe educational preparedness of a child. However it manifests it should be harnessed to improve understanding on the part of the teacher (or in my case the learner) to understand better how to connect with and motivate that child. Never be deflected from this as we as educationalists have, I believe, the responsibility to educate every single child, not just those who sit still and listen. I was fortunate to have trained at a time when the child was at the heart of learning and believing we should discover and use an individual child's strengths to invite and motivate them to discover 'learning; in all its guises. Today, since the introduction of the National Curriculum, which landed daily, in its many revised forms, on my headteacher's desk during the late 1980s, it is a requirement for schools to construct lists and content of subject defined blocks of learning to be mastered and to facilitate the assessment of an individual child's progress and ability. Yet this system fails many of our children. It sadly can misdirect schools into chasing league tables of scores which do not extend nor motivate the gifted nor identify the amazing talents and strengths of many on the autistic continuum.

My role has always been to motivate children and then later in my career adults – the team around and working alongside me. In 1985 in Berkshire, as a new and enthusiastic headteacher, I was given the opportunity to arrange a conference for all head teacher colleagues in the county with a focus on self appraisal. In doing so I had the unique opportunity to delve into systems used by the Civil Service, the army and a large notable corporation. I introduced a voluntary appraisal system the following year for any of my staff team who wished to help me develop this. To understand one's own personal strengths, and especially areas for development, and to discuss this openly with an empathetic colleague demands both the determination to improve and the humility needed to admit there is more to educating children than just providing information. I have always reflected on my own behaviour and communication. How should I approach a problem, a difficult pattern of behaviour, a child who is not motivated to learn. What am I doing wrong?

Certain elements of personal behaviour, particularly speech and posture, have a tremendous influence and effect on individual or groups of children. I initially realised that the consistency of my behaviour was imperative. I was lucky that I had worked for a headteacher who in all but one respect was incredibly successful and most of the children and staff benefitted from her passion and dedication. However she regularly lost her temper and reduced staff as well as children to tears. She was consistent because everyone in the school knew of this tendency and in an open plan environment we all heard the consequences. But I realised that 'fear' was the unintended consequence and I decided before becoming a head that I would discipline myself and use alternative strategies to gain the respect, understanding and educational excellence I wanted for all those in my care. All children need boundaries – right from wrong – and sadly some come to school with no concept of 'listening' which is such a necessary skill for achievement and discussion so that the children will have the capability of making good choices throughout their lives.

First, I worked on my voice. Being firm, consistent but above all calm was much more effective than shouting. I remember in the five years as head of the primary school I only ever shouted once – very loudly and with the whole school having been sent for and left standing apprehensively in the school hall. I made a quiet but dramatic entrance! What an impact that had. Afterwards I would hear children say to each other........Mrs Filley says! Interestingly it had been a social misdemeanour! We had five acres of beautiful school grounds plus a wonderful slope. During a snowy period I had asked the children not to build slides on the pavements outside school or near their homes in case elderly residents slipped and fell dangerously. Instead we allowed slides on the playground and polythene bags to be used on our grassy slope. But that day I had found out that an elderly lady had fallen and broken her leg on a slide built by some of our school pupils. That day they all learnt of my disappointment in them.

But in all other scenarios to lower your voice, even to a whisper, is so much more effective.

Earlier this current year I was invited by the parents of an autistic seven year old to meet the family - mother, an army major, father and the two small boys. The local primary school was having difficulties managing the child's anxiety and resulting behaviours and he was having to be isolated more and more from his peers. He was energetic and often difficult to manage at home and father admitted frequently shouting at him but to no effect. During our conversation together I beckoned to the child to come and stand beside my chair which he did. I quietly said thank you to him and smiled. I carried on listening to the parents and occasionally looked down at the boy and whispered how pleased I was with him or asked him a question to which he replied. He stayed very close beside me even though his younger brother was trying to tempt him to play with him. I advised the parents to try and avoid any shouting and replace it with calm posture, little speech and to offer praise for even the smallest success (they realised I was demonstrating this to them.) In other words to model the behaviour you wanted to see your child use rather than a demonstration of personal lack of patience and control. Our discussions together allowed me to praise their son several times in front of them, always whispering to him, and show them that our own behaviour as adults must be measured and disciplined rather than frightening the son into obedience, which with an autistic child just will not work. When it was time to go the little boy followed me closely all the way to my car. He and I had made an important bond in a very short time. Unfortunately, the family moved because the mother was re-posted, but I would happily have worked with the school staff to use these tactics and they had kindly agreed to facilitate this.

So how did I always manage to control children, some of them the most difficult in each school I worked in throughout my career, since I had inevitably requested that they be a part of my class? Apart from lowering my voice when I needed to discipline it is important to remember that all the children in the group are watching intently how you, the teacher, are handling difficulties or problems. The most important discovery I made was how to use my eyes! In the world of autism eyes are probably the most effective form of communication between adult and child, especially if the facial expression gives no other emotional cue. It is important to remember that with any child your attention is the most important reward you can give. Some autistic children shun any eye contact, so other forms of posture and gesture become important to make and maintain contact with that child. But conversely the eyes and the messages they display have a definite influence on the child's behaviour. I have trained my eyes to be expressionless when necessary and with totally calm body posture and no speech at all I am able to reduce anxiety and challenging behaviour very quickly.

I can admit that distressed children always attract my attention and several times recently I have quietly gone up to a struggling adult and whispered who I am and a little of my background and enquired if I might help. Because I am whispering the child immediately ceases the screaming or tantrum, watching intently to try and find out who I am and why I am talking to their parent? The grateful parent simply says yes please and thankyou because public tantrums are always embarrassing to handle. I then bend down to the child's eye level and quietly say hallo. My eyes bear no expression, neither does my face and I am able to say to the child very quietly 'thank you for stopping screaming for me. Well done'. Then I smile at the child, stand up, say goodbye to them both and move away. The screaming has stopped and with no threats, punishments or shouting.

It really does work. You simply have to distract the child by doing and looking at something or somebody else. Start a conversation if you can. In other words do not let the child have complete control of you and that huge array of florid expressions we use to display our worry, anger, frustration, embarrassment and horror which we so often show. These adult behavioural responses may be just the outcome the child expects and needs to maintain his difficult behaviour. By remaining calm, and without displaying any emotion or facial gestures of disapproval, the screaming may cease almost instantly. Then you will be able to find something to quietly distract and offer praise and a smile.

In fact, as I have shared many times with colleagues, during an episode of challenging behaviour, spoken words should be as few as possible. They should contain no threats of outcomes, no mention of a 'naughty step' nor a star chart! These consequences are for sharing in the future. The only immediate objective is to contain and reduce the behaviour. The time to discuss any outcomes or consequences with the child (or the management team) should only happen once the behaviour has ceased and may even, for the child, be sometime or even a day later. But discussed it must be, and every single time. The one rule I have adopted is 'immediacy'. Every behavioural reaction must be consistently managed to avoid it being repeated and, in the worse case, becoming entrenched and obsessional.

This is a good principle to apply to any management situation as I share frequently with professional colleagues elsewhere! Never brush behaviours 'under the carpet'. This does not help the child to make progress. The only word I would not tolerate when making reference to behaviour of students at Hope Lodge was 'naughty'. In fact any negativity demonstrated by an adult resulted in an escalation of physical behaviours. Whereas calmness, patience and then always taking time to reflect and understand what had happened will help staff and the child make better choices next time. Our intent was to enable every student to understand and control their anxieties themselves.

Tone of voice and respecting the child, even when behaviours are challenging, is really important and helps quickly establish a bond of trust. One or two of the children would come to me after an incident to talk through what had happened. They were not 'sent' to me as a punishment but rather as a respectful way of helping them develop confidence in verbalising their anxiety and finding positive ways of influencing their future reactions. I had initially on joining the school team to accept that the children all called me Mrs Filley, whereas all other staff members were known to the children by their Christian names. The staff reasoned, and were quite correct in their insistence, that as the headteacher I was the ultimate authority for permission and discipline and the students should all understand this. I remember one occasion when visiting one of our residential sites one evening a student abruptly told me to get out and go back to the school. We agreed as a staff team I should appear frequently in all settings so that the students all understood my role covered all aspects of their life with us. I made sure to speak positively and frequently in all those settings with this young man so that he understood.

One student whose behaviour could be challenging was the extremely verbal student who wrote the poem and then the song 'Why?' She and I developed a specific response to any inappropriate behaviour. Sometime after an incident when she was calm she would be given time by her class teacher to discuss what had happened with me. Because she was so articulate she could remember and describe the antecedents causing the problem and these we recorded, either in words or pictorially. She was very honest and self-critical and this process might engage us for up to an hour. During our discussions we both suggested alternative reactions to what she had experienced. These she also captured in words or drawings. At the end of this process we both quite formally decided the most appropriate choice of behaviour if similar circumstances happened again. I recorded these – as a formal contract between the two of us. She then went back to class and I asked my secretary to type up the contract. There were spaces for both of us to sign and at the end of the day she collected and kept the contract as a reminder for the future. She could even take this paper home and involve her parents in the discussions and outcomes. In this way we all showed absolute respect for her inability to cope in a specific scenario, gave her quality time when she was calm to talk this through and suggest healthy alternative behaviours for her to rehearse and use the next time those circumstances occurred.

This patient and positive way to improve her behaviour was really successful. No sending her out of a room, segregating her from others at meal times, or other form of negative language or outcome. Positive intervention really does work. I used this strategy for several other students at Hope Lodge where it was appropriate.

It is always important to be aware of the language you use to children, but especially in the case of an autistic child. For these children language should be simple, logical and without emotional content. This will help establish a communication bond which in turn will increase the child's ability to react appropriately. Talking through possible choices quietly, and where possible using visual cues, will in turn reduce anxiety in the child. They begin to have control over outcomes – and their own future. Understanding that they cannot always control and have the response they want or need helps them cope with the greatest common issue for them all – change.

I was walking a small group of children from the Language Unit towards the Gosport Ferry terminal. Our trip for the day was a short ferry ride across the river to Old Portsmouth and its interesting sights. I was holding Martin's hand – he being the most unpredictable child in the group. Suddenly, just prior to the ticket office, he let go of my hand, jumped ahead and lay down on the pavement facing me. His hands were held together in front of him as if in prayer. He looked up at me and said 'Disneyland Paris. Please Mrs Filley. Disneyland Paris'. I of course had to gently disappoint him and explain that today our ferry journey was a short one just across the river. I apologised to him and also explained those were the wonderful trips that only his parents could give him and perhaps he would like to ask them to take him there again one day. I was so proud of him, and told him so as he slowly got up and held my hand again. But he continued to gaze at my face in case he could see me changing my mind. He had asked me to change and I could not, but with quiet explanation from me he had already learnt to respect what I said to him. No tantrum, which was a huge improvement for both his level of tolerance and his need to control all outcomes. I had seen photographs of his trip with him standing with Goofy and Minnie Mouse, so I understood why he would want to influence our trip that day!

I was fortunate in the fact that my own secondary school – Dartford Girls Grammar School – had the motto...............In quietness and confidence. That has definitely influenced my life and my professional career. The down side to that part of my life was that I never met nor even knew that Mick Jagger was at the nearby boy's grammar school at the same time! He later donated funds for his old school to establish a department for drama and entertainment.

Being able to cope with difference and changes in timetable was a very important aspect of our work with our students as this is a huge area of difficulty and intolerance for autistic children. Every form of communication, especially picture cues, charts and daily timetables were shown to and discussed with individuals or class groups and sometimes change was introduced quite deliberately to exploit the students' hyper-sensitivity to this. As students progressed they themselves as a group might suggest changes. This was so important for those students who would go on to lead more independent life styles, but of course it helped all the students cope with changes without resorting to behaviour which was difficult for both themselves and for others to manage.

One particular Friday the most dramatic change was to affect us all without warning! An unexpected test for students and especially for the staff, in fact in everyone's ability to manage sudden change in routine, expectation and events. And all to be achieved calmly.

Traditionally, on a Friday it was always fish and chips for lunch, prepared by our own chef and her team and cooked on the premises, with of course the usual choice of alternatives for students who could not eat these items. Suddenly an emergency caused the biggest single change for us all to deal with.

Someone reported a smell of burning from a cupboard housing our main source of electricity. We constantly had washing machines, spin driers as well as technical facilities in use. My office was above this room so I pressed the fire alarm and called my secretary to summon the fire brigade. I then rushed down stairs with others to see a thin wisp of smoke coming through a small gap in the cupboard door. My role was importantly to ensure compliance with the process of evacuating all buildings and so complete our procedures (often rehearsed with the students) for the safety of children and staff. But it was eleven o'clock. Cook had been part way through the morning's preparations for the beloved fish and chips!

The Fire Brigade attended very quickly and took some time to correct and then repair the damaged power source. The students, dutifully lined up in their allotted class evacuation places at the far side of the playground, were then rewarded. When all was safely restored to full working order, the Fire Officers talked to them, showed them their equipment and when it was safe to do so took them to visit the fire engine. So a very successful test of our procedures with a bonus for the students.

Or was it? No, because it was then nearly twelve o'clock. Lunch time. During the time outside much quietly shared discussion had taken place without the students' knowledge between me, cook and a few staff standing close by. We concocted a very different lunch time for the students and as soon as we could we put it into practice. Fast!

The children were escorted back to their classrooms having obviously quite enjoyed the excitement of the unusual morning's timetable. The class teachers all warned the students that lunch time would be different too because cook had not been able to prepare their favourite menu.

BUT they were delighted to hear they would still have fish and chips! A second change we had all hurriedly agreed was inevitable was that the dining room had not been prepared for the meal with tables and chairs set out as usual and there was now no time for that to happen. So lunch would be taken in the class-rooms though still served by the cook and her team. A fish and chip picnic!

Quietly behind the scenes my secretary had warned our local fish and chip shop of our desperate need and they looked after us wonderfully well. We were given top priority by them straight away for which we were so grateful. Several staff were despatched to collect the food and bring it back to the school. Cook and her team distributed cutlery, plates and then the food to each class. Because the staff team were all so efficient this new drill happened smoothly and quickly and was greeted by the students' smiling faces and happy gestures of approval.

The whole incident was unexpected, a huge challenge, with considerable changes for students and staff. Amazingly it was enjoyed by all.....except one student! He sought me out and said very seriously to me – 'Mrs Filley that must never happen again'. I apologised to him but said that unfortunately I could not make such promises to him. I told him I understood it had been difficult for him to make the sudden changes but I was so proud that he had managed to do this. He was content with this positive praise and went quietly back to his classroom.

Once again the strength we had as a team, which I am sure we were able to share and use positively to influence our students, was our calmness, no matter what was happening. I will repeat – with autism it is imperative never to be surprised and always to remain calm and patient.

As I write these thoughts we are all experiencing monumental changes to our routines and thoughts for the future. As a nation we are having to cope with the isolation and changes imposed on us, our families and our routines because of Covid 19. How are autistic people and especially children dealing with this? Mark has told me that he is fine. He is ringing his mother in Tenerife everyday to make sure she and his step father are safe and well. He is taking two walks for exercise each day, maintaining his laundry, housework and shopping routines and is watching and enjoying his collection of DVDs in the extra time since he cannot work in his charity shop. Well done Mark.

A friend has a son who requires a high level of support and has, since leaving his specialised secondary school, had a number of adult placements which have been unsuccessful in meeting his complex needs. His current placement is very successful, which is a joy for the mother, especially in these restricted times when she cannot get her weekly hug...............a joy for her but she thinks not necessarily so for her son! It was his birthday two weeks ago and she handed his birthday cake over to staff through a window and has currently to be content that her weekly visits are simply gestures and shared thoughts through the glass. However she has happily shared his 'lockdown' and isolation routine with me. It is very different from his normal timetable that he readily knows and accepts. But she understands he has made the transition to the new routines remarkably well for which she is grateful. It includes the following:

9.00 Joe Wicks – on-line;

11.00 Strictly Come Dancing therapy session – on-line;

12.00 Cookery;

13.00 Exercise outside;

15.00 College work;

17.00 Connection with his family, either through a window or using Skype

This is a very different timetable for the young man, but necessary to avoid as much contact with others as possible whilst satisfying the need for a varied and fulfilling day for him.

Autistic children are special and it has been my privilege to work with them, their families and many gifted, patient and courageous staff so that 'together' we discovered the myriad of talents, infinite reliability, honesty and above all a memory for even the most insignificant of detail. You should always pick an autistic person to be your partner for Trivial Pursuits!

I am honoured that family, friends and colleagues have all spurred me on to complete this snap shot account of a very fulfilling professional journey with its focus on my time well-spent in listening and learning from those diagnosed with autism or Asperger Syndrome. The fact that they receive special education is in my view not because of any lack or deficiency in them but in the inability of the majority of us to accommodate and understand their gifts. If shown empathy, patience, calmness and above all infinite personal discipline on the part of those of us given the privilege of working with and supporting them, these young people are capable of so much more than we expect or imagine. As a headteacher of a mainstream school my aim was to discover and unlock the personal talents of each individual child. I took this rationale with me into the 'special' world of autism and have been so rewarded by all I have learnt about them whilst aspiring to the same dedicated personal and professional intent.

They and their families have taught me so much more about how best children learn. I would wish for the future that the understanding of emotional well-being and happiness could underpin our educational system so that we truly engage with and motivate all children. Sitting still in rows does not constitute good behaviour. It is simply compliance with restrictions. I know too many bright children and adults who are, or have been, totally bored and switched off from what we currently offer as an educational experience for all -which is far too restrictive in my view.

All autistic children can and should be offered the right to ever broader experiences and opportunities for a happy and fulfilling life. They have so much to contribute to all our lives.

References:

BLUER D.V.M (1916) Lehrbuch der Psychiatrie in FRITH U ed (1991) Autism and Asperger Syndrome. Cambridge, Cambridge University Press

CRYSTAL D (1976) Child Language Learning and Linguistics. London, Edward Arnold

HARRIS (1990) Early Language Development. London, Routledge

KANNER L (1943) Autistic Disturbances of Affected Contact in FRITH U (1989) Autism, Explaining the Enigma. Oxford, Blackwell

OFSTED Report Hope Lodge School (September 2001) Reference number: 116572

SYLVIA K and LUNT I (1982) Child Development, A First Course. Oxford, Blackwell

Warnock Report   (Special Educational Needs)
(1978)   Report of the Committee of Enquiry into
the Education of Handicapped Children and Young
People, Chairman, Mrs HM Warnock.   London,
Her Majesty's Stationary Office